WHAT ARE VIRUSES?

T0364411

Contents

Written by Isabel Thomas

Collins

What are viruses?

Viruses are very small **germs** – too tiny to see
with our eyes. This photo was taken by
a powerful **microscope**. You could line up
10,000 of these viruses on a full stop.

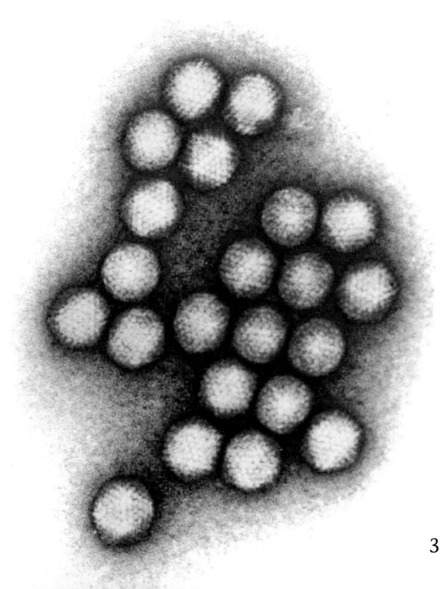

What's the difference between viruses and other germs?

Viruses are much smaller
than other germs.
But that's not
the only difference.

Germs such as **bacteria**
are living things.
They move, feed, grow, get
rid of waste and make
copies of themselves.
When they do these things
inside our bodies, they can
make us ill.

Viruses are not alive.
They don't move, feed
or grow. But some viruses
can cause illnesses if they
get inside a living thing.

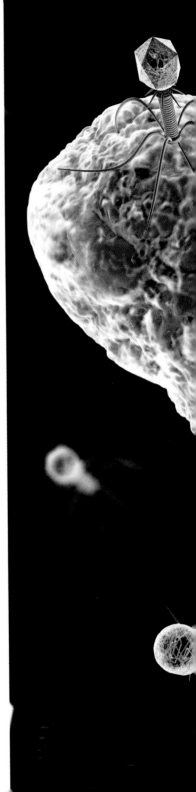

4

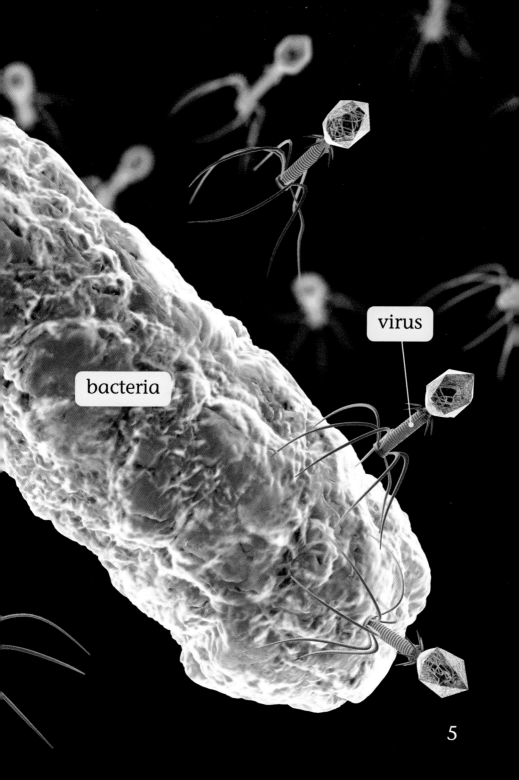

virus

bacteria

How many types of viruses are there?

There are probably *billions* of types of viruses: too many for scientists to count!

All viruses have:

- instructions for building new viruses
- a protective coat.

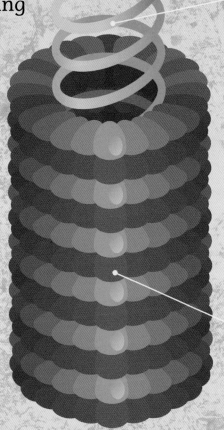

Some viruses are long and thin.

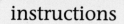

instructions

coat

Some have a head and tail.

Some look like spheres.

7

What do viruses actually do?

Viruses can't do anything on their own! They can't move or feed. They can't make copies of themselves.

Everything changes when viruses gets inside living cells, the building blocks of all living things. Viruses trick cells into doing all the jobs they can't do on their own!

Some viruses only infect **microbes**. Some only infect plants.

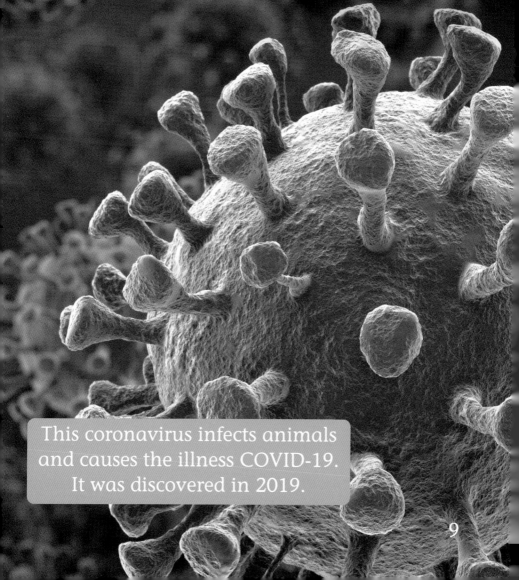

How do viruses get into a cell?

A virus can only invade a cell if it has the right "key" to fit a "lock" on the cell. Only about 200 types of viruses can get inside human cells and make us ill. Most viruses are not harmful to humans.

This coronavirus infects animals and causes the illness COVID-19. It was discovered in 2019.

How do viruses make us ill?

Viruses turn cells into virus factories. They trick the cell into making thousands of new viruses. The new viruses break out and spread to other cells. These cells become virus factories too. This can damage our cells or stop them from working properly.

Under a powerful microscope, we can see purple flu viruses breaking out of a human cell.

Can viruses change your skin colour?

Many viruses cause a rash. Sometimes this is because the virus has invaded the patient's skin cells. Sometimes it's a sign that the patient's body is busy fighting the virus.

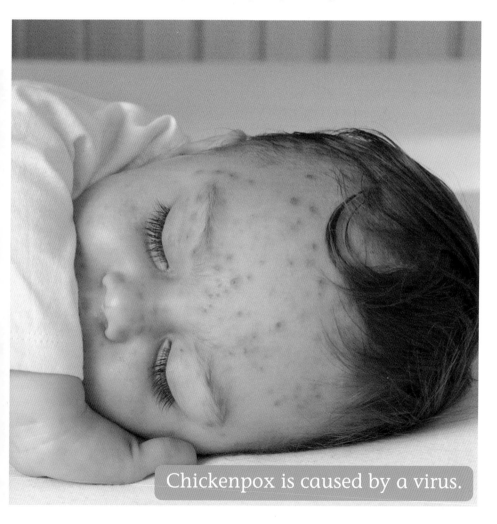

Chickenpox is caused by a virus.

How do our bodies fight viruses?

Our bodies have tough defences to keep viruses out.

tears

snot

saliva

skin barrier

If a virus does get in, our **immune system** gets to work. It tracks down cells with a virus inside and destroys the virus. This causes some of the **symptoms** of infections. Medicines and rest can help us feel better until our immune system has beaten the virus.

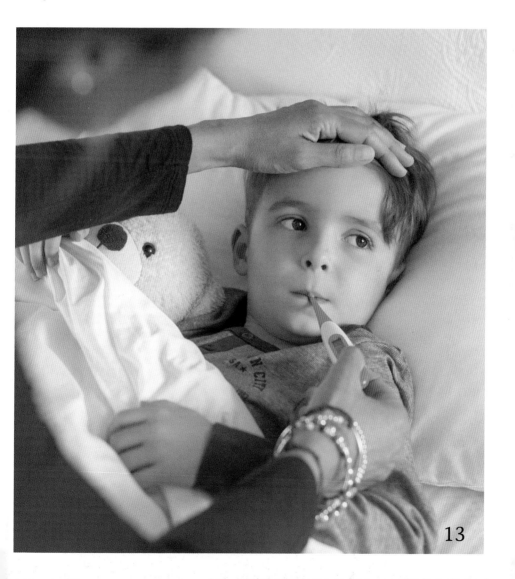

How do viruses spread?

Different viruses spread in different ways.

Cold viruses invade cells in our nose
and throat. This causes us to make LOTS of
extra snot and sneeze more often. Each time we
sneeze, thousands of droplets rush out.
Each droplet is packed with millions of viruses.

The droplets leave our nose faster than a car
travels on a motorway. Some land on food,
objects and surfaces. Some hang about in
the air. Other people breathe them in.
Now the viruses are inside a new person.

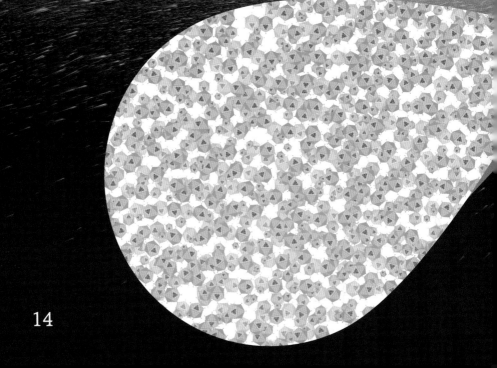

OK, how do we stop viruses spreading?

If you have an illness caused by a virus, such as a cold, there are things you can do to stop the virus spreading.

1. Stay at home while you have symptoms.

2. Put something over your mouth and nose when you sneeze or cough.

3. Put used tissues straight in the bin.

4. Wash your hands often. Soap, water and scrubbing can break viruses apart.

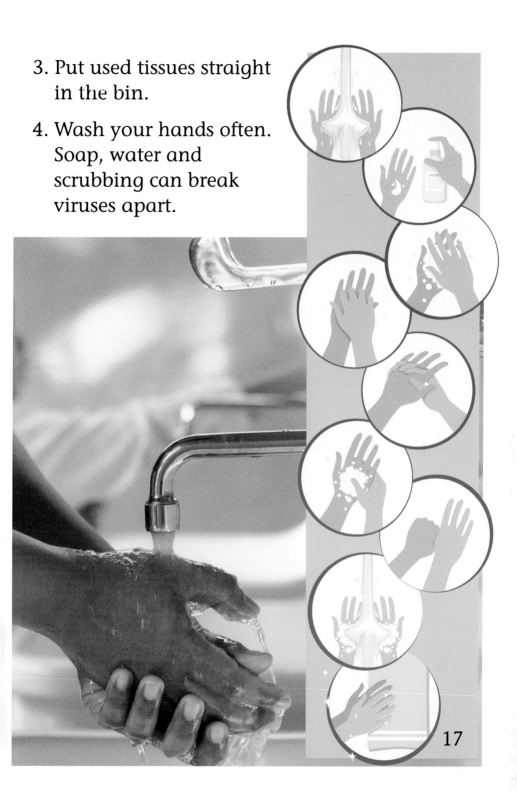

Can we get rid of viruses forever?

Once you have had a virus, your immune system remembers how to fight it. If the virus gets inside your body again, your body beats it so quickly you don't get ill. You are immune!

Can we become immune without having to get ill first?

This is exactly what vaccines do! A vaccine teaches your immune system how to fight a virus.

Each vaccine can only teach your body to fight one kind of virus.

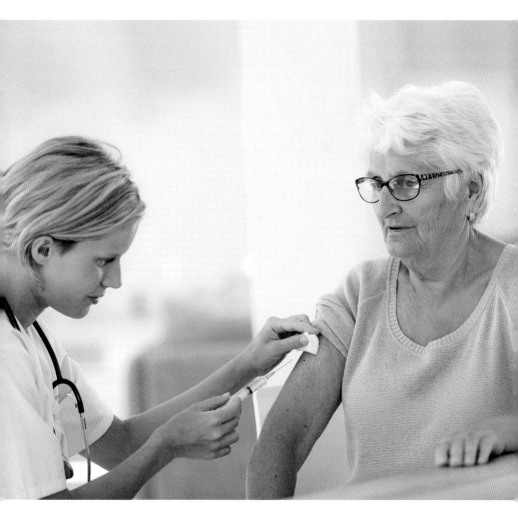

There are lots of different kinds of flu virus, so people who need a flu vaccine get a different one each year.

What if there were no viruses?

Viruses can have a devastating impact, as seen during the Covid-19 pandemic. They can cause loss of life, and also change the way that we live our normal lives.

A world without viruses sounds good, but viruses are very important. They can be used by doctors and scientists, to make vaccines, and to carry missing instructions into cells that aren't working properly.

Some viruses may even help to keep us healthy by activating our immune systems, and even fighting harmful bacteria!

Now I know what viruses are!

Glossary

bacteria tiny living things; if they live on or in our bodies, some bacteria can cause diseases

germs another name for tiny living things that cause diseases

immune system all the part of a person's body that work together to help prevent and fight diseases

microbes tiny living things that are too small to see without a microscope

microscope an instrument that makes tiny things look bigger, so that we can see them

symptoms the signs that a person has a disease, such as a cough, rash, pain or fever

Index

21

Virus-vanquishing toolkit

Your immune system

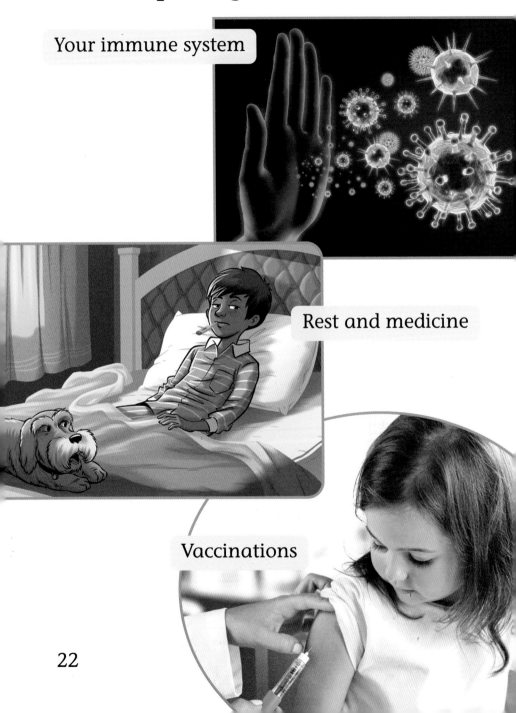

Rest and medicine

Vaccinations

Catch it!
Bin it!

Wash your hands!

23

 Ideas for reading

Written by Christine Whitney
Primary Literacy Consultant

Reading objectives:
- discuss how items of information are related
- be introduced to non-fiction books that are structured in different ways
- discuss and clarify the meanings of words

Spoken language objectives:
- ask relevant questions
- speculate, imagine and explore ideas through talk
- participate in discussions

Curriculum links: Science: the importance for humans of hygiene; Writing: write for different purposes

Word count: 839

Interest words: bacteria, virus, germs, immune system, defences, microscope, symptoms

Resources: paper, pencils and crayons or paints

Build a context for reading

- Ask children to talk to each other about being ill. How did they feel? What were the symptoms? Support children with their understanding of the word *symptoms*.
- Read the title of this book together and discuss what children think a virus is. Encourage them to ask any questions they have about viruses. Keep these questions and see if they are answered by reading the book.
- Read the blurb on the back cover of the book. Ask children to explain to each other what a *microscope* is. Has any child used a microscope before?

Understand and apply reading strategies

- Read pages 4 and 5 and ask children to name two differences between viruses and germs.
- Continue to read to page 12. Ask children to explain how our bodies fight viruses. They should use the following words in their answers: *tears, saliva, snot, skin barrier*